SPOT THE
DIFFERENCE

SPOT THE
DIFFERENCE

can you find them all?

Sean Keogh

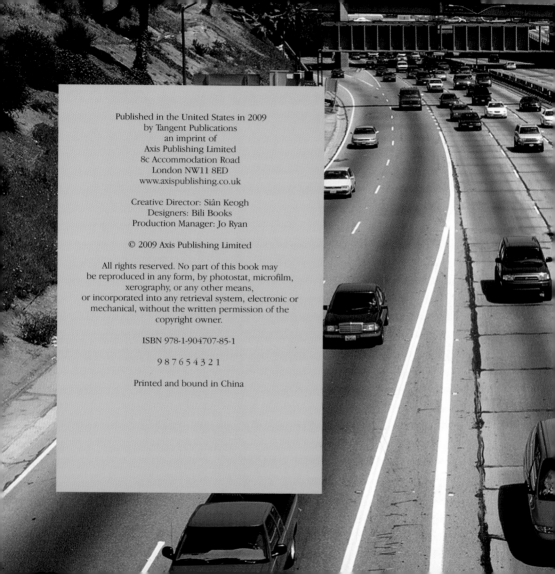

Published in the United States in 2009
by Tangent Publications
an imprint of
Axis Publishing Limited
8c Accommodation Road
London NW11 8ED
www.axispublishing.co.uk

Creative Director: Siân Keogh
Designers: Bili Books
Production Manager: Jo Ryan

ISBN 978-1-904707-85-1

9 8 7 6 5 4 3 2 1

Printed and bound in China

THE PUZZLES

spot 6 differences

spot 8 differences

spot 6 differences

spot 8 differences

spot 6 differences

spot 6 differences

spot 8 differences

spot 6 differences

spot 8 differences

spot 8 differences

spot 6 differences

spot 8 differences

spot 6 differences

spot 8 differences

45

spot 8 differences

spot 10 differences

spot 6 differences

spot 8 differences

spot 8 differences

spot 8 differences

spot 6 differences

spot 6 differences

spot 6 differences

spot 6 differences

spot 6 differences

spot 6 differences

spot 8 differences

spot 6 differences

spot 6 differences

THE ANSWERS

answers 24 & 25